PERRY ELEMENTARY SCHOOL
LIBRARY

SHAFTSBURG
ELEMENTARY LIBRARY

SHAFTSBURG
ELEMENTARY LIBRARY

The Making of a Detective

ALSO BY ROBERT H. MILLIMAKI

FINGERPRINT DETECTIVE

The Making of a Detective

Robert H. Millimaki

J. B. LIPPINCOTT COMPANY   PHILADELPHIA AND NEW YORK

I'd like to thank the Federal Bureau of Investigation for the use of their photographs, and particularly the staff of the National Academy for the training which helped make this book possible. My thanks also to detectives Bill Knox, Joe Semasko, and Bill Zorzy for their assistance in illustrating this book.

U.S. Library of Congress Cataloging in Publication Data

Millimaki, Robert H
  The making of a detective.

  Includes index.
  SUMMARY: Description of detective work with cases to illustrate aspects of the job.
  1. Detectives—Juvenile literature. 2. Criminal investigation—Juvenile litera-
ture. [1. Detectives. 2. Criminal investigation] I. Title.
HV7922.M53   364.12′023   76-8519
ISBN-0-397-31694-1

COPYRIGHT © 1976 BY ROBERT H. MILLIMAKI
ALL RIGHTS RESERVED
PRINTED IN THE UNITED STATES OF AMERICA
FIRST EDITION

TO BOBBY, FUTURE SPECIAL AGENT
CLASS OF '95

Contents

1. The Making of a Detective

HOW MANY TIMES have you watched a detective on a TV program examine the scene of a crime, pick up and handle different objects, stick a pencil in the barrel of a gun, or walk around the scene as if he were on tour? Probably hundreds of times. Fortunately, this type of investigation at a crime scene isn't often practiced by real detectives. These fictional detectives are destroying valuable evidence such as fingerprints, striation markings (microscopic scratches) on the weapon, and any number of other clues that could aid the investigator.

But not all fictional detectives set such a bad example. Sherlock Holmes could discover a startling amount of information about a complete stranger from a brief glance. By looking at a man's fingernails, the callouses on his hands, his shoes, and his clothing he could determine the man's occupation, personal habits, background, education, history, and much more. To many it seemed as though he could read their minds. But his ability was not based on any superhuman powers; instead, he relied on the observation of seemingly insignificant details. "You know my method," he once explained to Dr. Watson. "It has long been an axiom of mine that the little things are infinitely the most important."

Unlike Sherlock Holmes, today's real professional detective is not expected to solve cases merely by looking at the hands and clothing of suspects. But the power of observation is still an important part of a detective's makeup. The detective must know how to properly conduct a crime-scene investigation in order to be successful. He or she must try to answer the questions *who, what, when, where, how,* and *why.* Until they are answered satisfactorily, the investigation is incomplete. To find the answers, the detective needs to combine careful observation with a wide range of knowledge, abilities, and skills.

Determining *who* is the victim of the crime is usually simple enough. It could be the store owner who was robbed at gunpoint, the homeowner whose house was burglarized, or the narcotics addict who is both the offender, in possession of illegal drugs, and the victim, being destroyed by the drug habit.

Establishing the identity of the criminal is another matter, not always so simple. All of the expertise available in the police sciences is primarily directed to answering this one important question: Who committed the crime? Answering it may involve gathering all of the physical evidence available, questioning witnesses, sketching pictures, showing photographs of suspects (mug shots), and following up any leads that might make an identification possible.

What was the crime? If it was arson or vandalism, what was destroyed? If it was an assault, what was done to the victim? If it was a narcotics offense, what kind of drugs were involved? If it was a robbery, what was taken and what was the

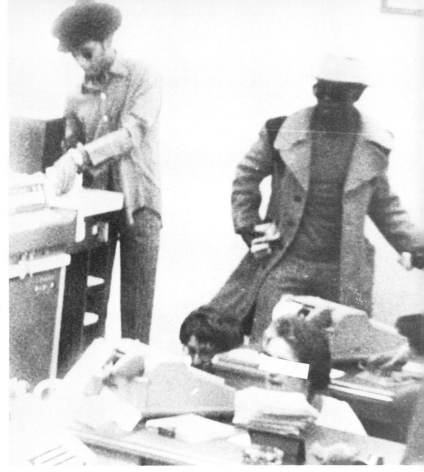

If you witnessed this actual robbery taking place, could you describe the robbers later? Study the picture for a minute or two, then see if you can remember five identifying features about each man. (Think about height, weight, build, clothing, weapons.)

monetary value of the items? This often determines whether the offense is classed as a misdemeanor, punishable by up to one year in jail, or as a felony, with a possible sentence of a year or more.

When did the crime occur? Usually this question can be answered by the victim, but not always. For example, the murder victim can't very well furnish this information, at least directly. Here is where the detective must have knowledge of the changes that take place in the body after death. How fast does rigor mortis (stiffening of the body) set in, and what parts of the body are affected first? How fast does blood dry at room temperature? What color is it after a few minutes or a few hours? What causes postmortem lividity (purplish coloring that appears on a dead body), and how fast does it occur? Knowing these answers helps the detective determine when the crime occurred.

Where was the crime committed? In most cases it happened right at the scene where the detective has been sent to investigate. Sometimes, however, a murder victim has been moved from the scene of the slaying to another location. The detective must consider whether the circumstances match the surroundings. Is the body in a position that fits in with the conditions at the scene? If the body shows signs of a struggle, is this reflected in the surroundings? Only close observation can lead to an accurate mental reconstruction of the crime.

How was the crime committed? What was the particular technique used? Were there any special quirks or peculiarities that make it stand out from other crimes in the same category? These peculiarities or special techniques are called the M.O., which stands for modus operandi, or method of operation. For example, not every robbery with a gun is committed the same way. One robber might walk into a liquor store and fire a shot into the floor or ceiling to show he means business. Another might not even take the gun out of his pocket. One might use a shotgun and wear a mask over his face, another a handgun and no mask. Some robbers are extremely nervous, while others are cool as icicles. Some are apologetic in their manner, while others will shoot their victims out of pure viciousness. Even the type of business a robber selects as his target can become a habit. Habit is often the robber's downfall. During the course of an investigation, the detective searches the M.O. files. If the criminal has been arrested before, his name and a description of his method of operation are likely to be found in these files.

Finally, *why* was the crime committed? Sometimes the answer can only be guessed at. But the reason why it was committed can often indicate what kind of person to look for as a suspect. For example, in a series of arson cases the detective will often take photographs of the spectators. Why? Because the pyromaniac (a person who compulsively sets fires) is usually a neurotic who follows a ritualistic pattern of behavior and is often a part of the crowd, possibly even helping put out the fire. If one particular face shows up at the scenes of a series of fires, that is a likely suspect and worth checking out.

In order to answer the questions *who, what, when, where, how,* and *why,* the detective must be trained to know the law, be a skilled technician, and conduct chemical tests. Detectives must be able to recognize, collect, and preserve the evidence at a crime scene: they must know the value of fingerprints, blood, chemicals, glass, firearms, toolmarks, wood, metals, explosives, photographs, documents, shoe prints, tire treads, soils, hair, and know how to secure information from them to aid in investigations. They must be acquainted with the techniques of dusting for latent (invisible) fingerprints, casting footwear and tire tread prints, sketching crime scenes, and taking photographs. They must be able to talk to people in all walks of life and obtain information from them. A detective must have an open mind, patience, and perseverance, and must be a team worker.

No one is born a detective. It takes training over a long period of time to acquire all the specialized skills and knowledge a good detective needs. But nothing learned is ever wasted. Good detectives go on learning as long as they go on working. The next case might require a knowledge of art or a familiarity with a zoo keeper's duties. That's one of the reasons a detective's job is always fascinating. Every case is a new puzzle, with new challenges to your wits and experience.

But all the specialized training would be wasted if the detective were not a skilled observer. Why is the art of observation so important? Simply because at the start of an investigation no one can tell what may turn out to be an essential clue. It might be a cigarette butt, a broken piece of glass, a missing button, or any number of things. You may discover its value as a clue only as you proceed with the investigation. Many times clues are overlooked and the crime remains unsolved. That's why care at the initial crime scene investigation and accurate observation are so vital to the detective.

People can be trained to be good observers. There are many ways to improve your powers of observation. One way is to study a strange room or a window display for a few minutes. Try to notice everything about it you can, then walk away. Next, write down everything you can recall: the placement of chairs, tables, windows, dishes, anything that comes to mind. Then go back and see how many errors you made or how many items you forgot to include. With practice, you'll find your powers of observation improving rapidly.

What about trying a short test now? All you'll need is a piece of paper and a pen or pencil. Study the illustration of the crime scene. Pay close attention to details and to anything that looks odd or out of place. Allow yourself five minutes to study the photograph. Then, without looking at the picture, see if you can answer the following questions about it.

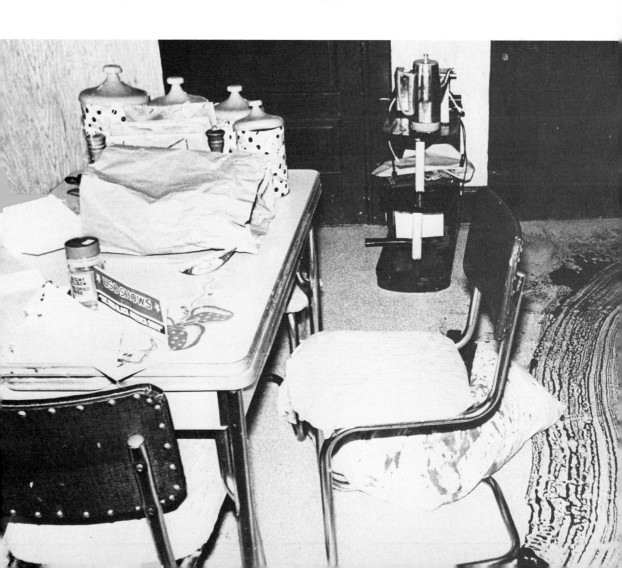

1. What kind of room is it?
2. What shape is the table?
3. Is there a coffeepot in the picture? If so, where is it?
4. Is there an unusual object in the room? What is it?
5. Is there a hammer? If so, where is it?
6. Where is the knife in the picture?
7. How many doors are in the picture?
8. How many canisters are on the table?
9. How many chairs are in the picture?
10. Was the pillow placed on the floor before the slaying or after? How can you tell?

Check the answer section to see if your results are the same. If you answered all of the questions correctly, you are an excellent observer and have the makings of another Sherlock Holmes. If you missed more than three of the questions, you need a little more practice. But don't worry about it; you'll learn as you go along, working on the case problems that follow. Of course, reading this book won't make a real detective out of you, any more than reading a book about swimming will make a swimmer out of you. But it can help to make you more observant of the things around you, and you'll have some fun in the challenge of finding the physical clues and solving the cases that are presented.

As you've already noted, it takes more than observation of physical evidence to make a good detective; but without knowledge of the law and the rules of evidence, the best place to start detecting is with physical evidence. The advantages are obvious. Physical evidence doesn't lie, it doesn't make judgments based on looks or personality, it speaks for itself.

It not only helps convict the guilty, it exonerates the innocent. If a picture is worth a thousand words, physical evidence is worth a thousand eyewitnesses.

So let's suppose you are allowed to be a detective for a few days, investigating crime scenes, searching for clues, learning as any detective does, by doing. Do you think you've got the makings of a detective?

The photographs in this book—except those used to illustrate certain points such as fingerprint patterns or matching fragments—are of actual criminals and crime scenes. The cases are based on actual crimes. The names and places have been changed, but they are representative of the situations and problems you are likely to encounter as a cadet detective.

2. A Case of Observation

YOU'VE BEEN TOLD by the chief of police to report to the detective bureau at eight o'clock Monday morning. There, Detective Jim Brogan is to be your assigned partner for the next three days. You've also been told that you're expected to carry your own weight. If you goof up, or can't take it, out you go, the same as any other police officer trying to make the grade of detective.

Now, at seven thirty Monday morning, you feel a little apprehensive as you walk into the police station. The uniformed officers are booking a prisoner, clerks are busily filing reports, the dispatcher is giving instructions in code numbers on the police radio, and a stern-looking sergeant is standing behind the information counter looking at you as if you'd intruded on a private meeting of some kind.

"Can you tell me where I can find Detective Brogan?" you ask.

"I might at that," he answers, "if you'll be telling me your business."

"I'm supposed to meet him. I'll be working with him a few days," you say proudly.

Suddenly it seems as if all the activity has stopped and everyone's eyes are on you. The room seems warmer somehow as the sergeant looks at you across the counter, a puzzled expression on his face.

"The Chief said I was supposed to report to Detective Brogan," you add quickly.

"Oh?" the sergeant asks. "Oh, yes," he goes on, apparently remembering. "You're the kid that got special permission from the Chief. Just a minute, I'll see if Brogan has come in yet." He turns to pick up the phone on the desk behind him.

As he dials the interoffice number you glance around the room and see that all the people are still busy with their own concerns. The feeling that they were all watching you was just in your imagination.

The sergeant speaks briefly on the phone, then turns back to you. "Just be following the hallway down to the second door on your left. That's the detective bureau, also sometimes called the smart shop. You'll find Brogan in there, likely as not with his feet on a desk and a cup of coffee in his hand."

"Thanks," you answer, heading in the direction the sergeant indicated.

At the door marked Detective Bureau, you pause, looking through the glass. You can see four desks, filing cabinets, typewriters on stands, camera equipment, a large bookcase, and four men wearing suits. It looks like any ordinary office.

One of the detectives is standing at a filing cabinet looking through some records. Another is seated at a desk with his back to you, typing. The other two are standing next to one of the desks talking to each other. Every one of them seems to have a cup of coffee, either in his hand or on the desk.

You turn the doorknob and step into the room. The men all turn and look at you.

"Hi, come on in," the detective at the filing cabinet says, smiling. "You must be looking for Brogan."

"Yes, sir," you answer. "Is that you?"

The detective seated at the desk grins. "Nope, he just wishes he was." He gets up from his chair and reaches out a massive hand as he towers over you. "I'm Brogan, and you must be my new partner for the next few days."

"Yes, sir," you answer, shaking his hand, glad to be on the same side he is. He seems almost a foot taller than everyone else in the room and broad enough to fill up the doorway.

"These two fellas are detectives Billy Fisher and Tom Grady. The little fella here at the filing cabinet is Lieutenant Frank Martin. He's the boss."

"Hi," you answer, acknowledging the introductions. The door opens again and a slim, small woman comes in.

"And this is Detective Anita Smith. Don't let that pretty smile fool you, she's got a karate kick that'll knock out a mule."

"Hi," she says, reaching out her hand.

"This is all of our day shift crew," Brogan goes on. "There are other detectives working the evening tours. You'll probably meet them later. But now I suppose you're wondering what you're supposed to do."

"Yeah, sort of," you agree.

"Well, for the time being, just relax for a few minutes while I fill out the rest of this report, and then I'll show you around before we hit the road."

Photographs taken by hidden bank cameras can be reproduced on wanted bulletins to help identify passers of bad checks.

"Okay," you answer. You sit in a vacant chair next to Brogan's desk and glance through a thick file of wanted bulletins.

The lieutenant returns his attention to the filing cabinet, and Fisher and Grady return to their conversation. They are arguing about the legality of continuing the search of a car once it has been brought off the street into the station. Smith picks up a police report from one of the desks and leaves the office again.

A few minutes later, Brogan pulls the completed report

from his typewriter and puts it into a tray on his desk. "Let's go," he says, handing you a small note pad and a ball-point pen. "Put these in your pocket. You'll be needing them."

He shows you around the police station, the lockup, the bureau of identification, and the radio room and explains the various records that are kept and how they are used. But it's all too much to absorb in a few minutes, and you're glad when he suggests going out on the road.

In the plain, unmarked car, Brogan points out the police radio mounted in the glove compartment. He explains that each police car, marked or unmarked, has a number assigned to it. Yours is 655. He tells you to listen for any traffic (police calls) directed to car 655.

As you ride around listening to the calls, waiting for the number of your car to come up, Brogan starts to explain the meaning of the various code numbers that are used. But there are just too many to remember easily, and sometimes the voices are distorted and hard to understand. Then suddenly you hear the numbers "Six fifty-five" come out of the speaker.

"Answer it," Brogan says.

"What'll I say?" you ask.

"Just say, 'Six fifty-five.' Go ahead."

You release the catch to the glove compartment, slide the mike off its hook, and put it to your mouth, repeating the words.

"Six fifty-five, go to St. Mary's Hospital emergency room and take a shooting report," the dispatcher orders.

You've heard TV detectives say "Ten-four" many times, and

you know it means acknowledgement. "Ten-four," you answer, without being told. You replace the mike in the glove compartment as Brogan heads the squad in the direction of the hospital.

"I wonder what that's all about," you say.

"Your guess is as good as mine," he answers. "But anytime a shooting victim is brought into a hospital, they're required to notify the police. It is a little unusual to get this type of call so early in the morning."

A short time later, Brogan parks the squad in the hospital lot. As you head for the emergency room, he instructs you to take down the information in your notebook while he questions the shooting victim.

Inside, you learn the victim's name is Carl Lowry. The nurse lets you copy his address, age, and other information from the admitting form. She tells Brogan that Lowry is in one of the emergency cubicles waiting for treatment and directs you to him.

Pushing the curtain aside, you follow Brogan into the room. Lowry is lying on a treatment cot, groaning in pain. He is pale and perspiring. His right pants leg is slit open almost to the thigh, and there is a small bandage dressing covering the wound, about six inches above the knee. You can see a round hole in the slit pants leg, about two inches below the wound. There is a small dark circular area around it.

"I'm Detective Brogan, and this is my partner," he begins. He examines the bullet hole in Lowry's pants leg, pulling the material so the hole lines up with the wound. "Mind telling us what happened?"

23

"I'm not sure myself," Lowry answers, wincing in pain. You try to make notes of Brogan's questions and Lowry's answers. "I was just walking along on the sidewalk when suddenly a car with three or four guys in it pulled up and took a shot at me."

"Where was this?" Brogan asks.

"On Greenleaf, between Fifteenth and Sixteenth."

"Got any idea why it happened?"

"No. I haven't got any enemies, at least none that want to shoot me."

"Was there any argument, or were words exchanged between you before it happened?"

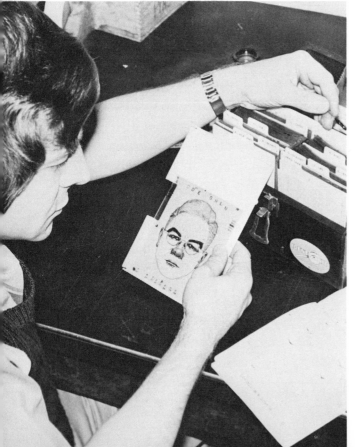

Detective Joe Semasko puts together an Identi-Kit composite portrait of a suspect from a description furnished by a crime victim. Each facial feature is on a separate transparent sheet, and different features are added until a satisfactory likeness is achieved.

"No. Like I said, they just pulled up next to the curb and took a shot at me, then took off."

"What did they look like?" you ask.

"I don't really know. It all happened so fast."

"Were they black, white, or what?" Brogan asks.

"White, I think."

"What about clothing? Can you describe what any of them was wearing?" Brogan continues.

"No. I don't think I'd know them if they walked in here right now."

"How about the car? Can you tell us anything about it?"

"No, not really. I guess I was too shocked to pay attention to it."

"Don't worry," you reassure Lowry. "We'll get the guys that shot you. Anybody that would—"

"Just a second," Brogan cuts in. He takes a small card out of his wallet and turns his attention back to Lowry. "Before I ask you any more questions, I've got to advise you of your rights."

"What for?" you blurt out, astounded.

"Yeah! I'd like to know myself," says Lowry.

"If you'll just hold on for a minute, I'll explain it to you," Brogan answers. He is speaking to Lowry, but he looks very sternly at you. His meaning is clear.

"First, you have the right to remain silent," he begins, reading from the card. "Anything you say can and will be used against you in a court of law. You have the right to an attorney, and if you can't afford one, the court will appoint one for you at no charge. You have the right to have your attorney present during questioning, and you can stop answering questions anytime you want. Do you understand these rights?"

"Sure," Lowry answers. "But I still don't get it."

"Are you willing to waive these rights before I go on with my questions?" Brogan asks.

"Sure, why not?" Lowry answers. "You must think I've done something. I'm curious to see what it is."

"You're right," Brogan says. "I'm going to have to charge you with making a false police report, but—"

"False police report?" you ask, amazed.

"As I was saying," Brogan goes on, giving you a sharp look. "But first I'd like you to tell me what really happened. You and I both know it's not what you've been telling us."

You can see that Lowry is as puzzled at the turn of events as you are. He seems to be weighing his answer in his mind.

"Okay, okay," Lowry answers finally. "It was an accident. I was sitting in my car with a buddy of mine and I showed him a pistol I'd just bought. He started to twirl it around on his finger, and the next thing I knew—blam, it went off. I just didn't want to get him in any trouble, so I made up the story."

"I thought it was something like that," Brogan says. "Where's the gun now?"

"In my car, under the seat. It's parked outside."

"How long have you had the gun?"

"Like I said, I just bought it the other day, brand new."

"Okay," Brogan answers. "I won't book you for transporting firearms, but you will be charged with filing a false police report. The charge is just a misdemeanor, and you'll be able to post a cash bond guaranteeing your appearance in court and be on your way in a short time. That is, if you'll consent to turning the gun over to me now so I don't have to bother with a search warrant."

"Go ahead and take it," Lowry answers. "I've had enough of guns for a while."

Later, having retrieved the gun from under the seat of Lowry's car, you are on the way back to the station to make out the report. You're still mystified at how things worked out. You're also a little worried that Brogan might be mad at you for opening your mouth at the wrong time. "I'm sorry about interrupting you like I did back there when—"

"Forget it this time," Brogan answers quickly. "I can see where you might have been surprised. Just so it doesn't get to be a habit."

"It won't," you say. "Still, I don't understand how you were so sure Lowry was lying about the shooting."

"Why not see if you can figure it out for yourself by answering a couple of questions. First, what happens to your pants legs when you sit down? Next, what do you think caused the dark circle around the bullet hole in the pants leg? Then ask yourself: When did the shooting happen, and why did it happen?"

When you think you've got the solution worked out, check the answer section and see if your explanation is similar to Brogan's.

3. A Burglary Investigation

YOU RETURN to the station so Brogan can type up the report on the shooting incident. Then you and he go to the hospital again a short time later to bring Lowry back for booking, fingerprinting, photographing, and posting his bond. This takes up most of the morning. There are still a lot of questions you want to ask Brogan about the investigation, but there just doesn't seem to be a time when he isn't busy. Finally, though, the paperwork is finished, and Lowry leaves the station with the aid of a crutch.

"How about lunch?" Brogan suggests.

"Sounds good," you agree.

Brogan turns to Lieutenant Martin just as the interoffice phone rings.

"Hold on a second," the lieutenant says, picking up the phone. You hear him tell whoever is on the line that he will send someone to the scene.

"Something tells me we're going to miss lunch," Brogan says.

"Sorry," the lieutenant says, hanging up the phone. "Grady and Fisher are out serving a warrant, and Smith is out running down a lead on that assault case from the other night.

You two are all I've got available. Your lunch will have to wait awhile."

"What've you got?" Brogan asks.

"Two-o-o-five Sutton. See a Mrs. Archer. The dispatcher says she just got home from shopping and found her house burglarized."

"Okay, we're on our way," Brogan says.

In the unmarked squad again, you turn to Brogan. "Could we stop for a sandwich before we go? I'm really hungry."

Brogan chuckles. "If we did that, I'd be back in uniform before morning. As it is, Mrs. Archer probably is already thinking it's taking too long for the police to get to her house. But I can drop you off and pick you up later if you want."

You can see Brogan is right, and if you don't go along, you might not get another chance to be in on a burglary investigation. "Never mind, I can wait. But what am I supposed to do when we get there?"

"Ever heard of the transfer theory?" Brogan asks.

"No, what's that?"

"Well," Brogan begins, "since we're investigating a burglary, we're going to try to answer the question, who did it? The transfer theory is one method of trying to answer it. It just means that anytime two objects come in contact with each other, each leaves some effect on the other that can be seen and examined. For example, you step on loose dirt; the pattern of your shoe is transferred into the soil, and some of the soil is transferred to your shoe."

"I get it," you reply. "Like, if I touch something with my fingers, I leave fingerprints on it."

"That's the idea," Brogan agrees. "Anytime you're investigating a crime of any kind, you're looking for clues left at the scene in four different ways. First, the criminal might leave clues from his body, such as fingerprints, teeth marks, blood, hair, and so on. Second, he might leave clues through his clothing, by glove prints, shoe prints, cloth, or fibers. Third, the weapons or tools he uses are another source of clues. A spent bullet, an empty cartridge casing, pry marks on wood or metal are some examples. The last way he might leave clues is through some physical act he committed, like tearing papers, writing a note, anything he does that alters the scene of the crime."

"It makes sense," you say.

"Not only does the criminal leave traces of himself in those four ways," Brogan continues, "but he can accidentally carry things away from the crime scene that can tie him in with it. The dirt he picks up on his shoes, insulation from a safe, slivers of glass from a broken window, blood from the victim, and many other things depending on the type of crime."

"I sure hope we can find something at this one," you tell Brogan as he slows down.

"Here we are," he says, pulling the car to the curb in back of a marked squad.

As you get out of the squad and walk up to the house, you see the uniformed patrolman step out, followed by a heavy-set, dark-haired woman. Her eyes look red, as if she has been crying.

"Hi, Brogan," the officer says. "This is Mrs. Archer. She

says she went out shopping a couple of hours ago and just got back and found her back door kicked in."

"What did they get, Mrs. Archer?" Brogan asks.

"Everything," she sobs. "My TV, the stereo, my best jewelry, everything. My bedroom is a mess."

"I've got a list of the items," the patrolman tells Brogan.

This is what Mrs. Archer found when she returned home. In their hurried search for valuables, the burglars simply emptied the drawers onto the floor.

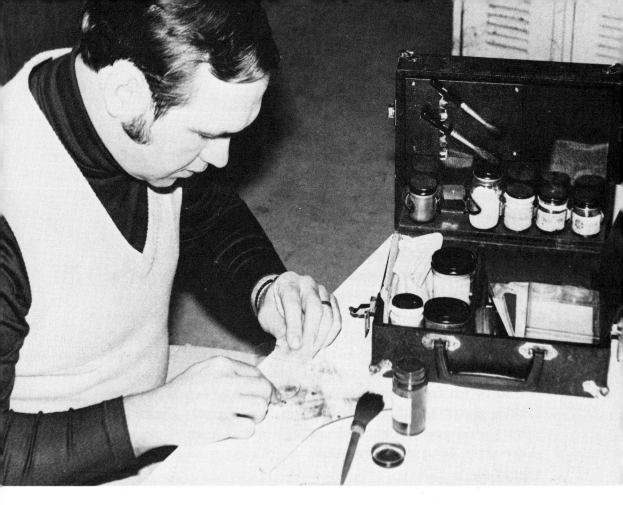

Detective William Zorzy places lifting tape over a latent fingerprint. It is then transferred to a plain white card.

"I will," you answer, heading for the first house directly across the street.

You ring the doorbell and wait impatiently for someone to answer it, but no one seems to be at home. You move down to the next house and ring the bell. Finally, an old, gray-haired man slowly opens the door.

"What is it?" he asks.

"Uh, I was wondering if you might have seen any cars or people at that house across the street," you answer, pointing at the Archer house. "They were burglarized a little while ago. I'm helping the police."

"What is this, some kind of joke?"

"No, sir, it's no joke. There was a burglary across the street and—"

"Okay, I heard you the first time. Burglary, huh?"

"Yes, sir. Did you see anything?"

"Not so fast, not so fast, I'm thinking," he answers, rubbing his chin thoughtfully. At least a full minute later the old man finally says, "Nope. Can't say that I did."

"Well, thanks anyway," you reply, disappointed, as you turn to leave.

"Unless . . ." the old man continues.

"Sir?"

"Well, I did see a kind of delivery truck parked in the drive over there not more than an hour ago. One of those panel trucks, I think."

"A delivery truck?" you ask.

"Yep. That's what I said."

"Well, I didn't mean anything like that," you tell him. "I meant somebody who looked suspicious."

"Sorry, that's the only thing I saw."

"Okay, thanks anyway," you answer, wishing he had come up with something useful.

35

You ring the bell of the house next door and again you get no response. You decide it's useless on this side of the street and run across to meet Brogan walking toward the squad.

"Any luck?" he asks as you join him.

"No," you say. "I didn't get any answer at two of the houses, and at the other one, all the guy saw was a delivery truck of some kind about an hour ago."

"He did?" Brogan asks, surprised. "Did you get a description of it?"

"Uh, no," you answer. "I didn't think there was anything suspicious about a delivery truck."

"Ordinarily there wouldn't be," Brogan explains. "But when a house has been burglarized while the owner has only been gone for two hours, any vehicle seen around it is suspicious, especially when large items like a TV and a stereo have been taken. It's obvious the burglar can't carry them on his back."

"Yeah. I guess I just wasn't thinking."

"Where does this man live?" Brogan asks. "We'll go back and talk to him again."

Returning to the house, Brogan questions the man and learns his name is Abe Summerford. Summerford tells Brogan the truck was dark green with a dent in the right rear fender. He describes the men in the truck as about twenty, wearing faded green coveralls. He also remembers the truck had the word "Hauling" printed on the side.

"Thank you," Brogan says. Together you head back across the street.

"I guess the next thing to do is put out a message on the police radio to look for the truck," you suggest.

"Not just yet. We'll check with Mrs. Archer first. The old man could be mistaken about the time the truck was there. Maybe she was home at the time, or knows who the truck belongs to. We don't want to waste time tracking down someone that might not have anything to do with the burglary."

"Yeah, I guess that makes sense," you agree.

Talking to Mrs. Archer again, Brogan asks her if she saw the two men and the truck in her driveway before she left the house.

"No," she answers. "But there were two men in a truck like that who stopped by just a few days ago. They asked me if I needed any trash hauled away. I told them no, and thought they were kind of suspicious, but they just thanked me and left. I didn't think any more about it. They parked out on the street, though, not in my driveway."

"Do you remember what the men looked like?" you ask, taking out your note pad again.

"Yes, I do," she answers. "They were both young, about nineteen or twenty. One of them was kind of heavyset, and short. He had light-colored hair, I think. The other had dark hair, and he was thinner."

"Do you remember anything about their clothes?" you ask, recalling the old man's description.

"Work clothes. Coveralls, I believe. Brown or green, I'm not sure."

"It's got to be the same guys," you tell Brogan.

"Sounds likely," Brogan answers, turning his attention

37

again to Mrs. Archer. "Thank you. Your description will help. As soon as we know something definite, we'll get in touch with you."

Returning to the station, Brogan goes over the notes you've taken, makes out a copy of the description, and gives it to the radio dispatcher. "Put out a local dispatch on this to our squads," he says.

Back in the detective bureau, Brogan removes the film from the camera and asks Lieutenant Martin to have Fisher develop it in the department photo lab as soon as possible, explaining that there is a heel print on it that may be of value. He also hands him the piece of broken glass in the plastic envelope. "There's a partial print on it, but I can't tell if it's of any value or not. You're the expert; I'll leave it up to you."

"Okay," Lieutenant Martin replies. "Got any other leads?"

"Just their descriptions and a description of the truck they used. There's a local dispatch out on it now," Brogan answers. "I was going to check the M.O. files to see if we can come up with a suspect."

"Good. Fisher's in the photo lab now. I'll have him get started on these pictures right away while you two check out the M.O. file."

A short time later, Brogan flips through the residential burglaries section of the file. He pulls out four cards and hands them to you. Each contains the name, address, and description of a suspect, and a summary of his burglary technique. "Which ones look the best to you?" he asks.

When you've examined the cards, check the answer section to see if your suspects match Brogan's.

```
BURGLARY  (House)              Kick in

BROWN, Alfred "Al"             CR#A-307295
1917 Market                    6-14-75
City
W/M   dob 5-3-54   5'10"   blk/hazel   155

House burglary, daylight.  Posed as roof
repairman.  Associate, Bernard Jones.
Photo B-387
```

```
BURGLARY  (House)              Kick in

CARPENTER, Roger               CR#A-300652
707 Kent                       5-7-73
City
W/M   dob 7-24-51   5'10"   lt. brn/blue   168
1" scar below right eye.

House burglary, daylight.  Posed as gas meter
inspector.  No known associates.
Photo C-1311
```

```
BURGLARY  (House)              Kick in

JONES, Bernard "Bernie"        CR#A-307295
1707 Akron                     6-14-75
City
W/M   dob 3-15-53   5'7"   bld/blue   190

House burglary, daylight.  Posed as roof
repairman.  Associate, Alfred Brown.
Photo J-137
```

```
BURGLARY  (House)              Kick in

MORLEY, Willie                 CR#A-297416
333 N. Bellow                  3-13-73
City
W/M   dob 12-1-52   6'   brn/brn   172

House burglary, daylight.  Checks house
by first ringing doorbell, looking for
fictitious person if answered.  No known
associates.
Photo M-621
```

4. The Proof

BROGAN COPIES DOWN the names and addresses of the four suspects, Brown, Carpenter, Jones, and Morley. "Let's check the bureau of identification and pull their pictures," he says. "Then we'll show them to Mrs. Archer and see if she can make an identification."

"How about their fingerprints?" you ask.

"You're catching on fast," Brogan says. "The lieutenant must have stepped out, but I'll leave a note on his desk to check out their prints too."

Brogan writes the note and pulls the pictures of all four suspects, plus a couple of extras. He puts 3″ x 5″ cards in the photo file with his initials on them to show he has taken the pictures out.

"Why did you take the extra pictures?" you ask.

"If I just showed Mrs. Archer the pictures of the men we suspect, it wouldn't be an identification we could use in court," Brogan explains. "The defense attorney would argue that we unduly influenced her identification, and it would be thrown out."

"I still don't see why."

PERRY ELEMENTARY LIBRARY

THE PROOF

"Well, there have been mistaken identifications before, and innocent people have gone to prison because of them. This is just one way to protect a person from that kind of mistake."

"Oh. I guess I can see that," you say.

"Good," Brogan answers. "You wouldn't want to have any doubts in your own mind if you were responsible for sending someone to prison, would you?"

"No, I wouldn't. I'd want to be sure."

"So would I," Brogan says, heading out to the squad.

As you are on the way to 2005 Sutton once more to show Mrs. Archer the photographs, the squad's radio catches your attention.

"Six forty-two, to any squads in the vicinity of Orchard and Carter. I'm in pursuit of a green panel truck; ten ninety-three suspects, headed north on Orchard."

"Hey!" you exclaim. "Did you hear that?"

"Yeah. Sounds like our burglary suspects have been spotted just a few blocks from here," Brogan answers. He reaches for the portable mars light on the seat, swings it out through the window so its magnetic base clamps onto the roof of the squad car, and plugs the cord into the cigarette lighter, all in one easy motion. "The red light will show the other traffic this is a police car. Hang on," he adds. The tires of the squad squeal as he takes a right turn, speeding up.

"Six forty-two, I'm now heading west on Lake Street, approaching Main," says the radio. You can hear the siren of car 642 in the background of the radio transmission. Brogan flips a switch under the dash, and a moment later the sound of the siren from your own squad is deafening.

41

"Turn the volume up on the radio," Brogan shouts. "We're getting close."

He turns left, the tires screeching on the pavement again. "They should be the next block over," he says.

The needle of the speedometer jumps from thirty to sixty. Brogan passes the slower-moving traffic as if it were standing still. "Hand me the mike," he shouts.

Caught up in the excitement of the chase, you fumble for it, trying to get it out of the glove compartment as 642 transmits again.

"Six forty-two, still westbound on Lake, about two blocks from Main."

Grabbing the mike off its hook, you hand it to Brogan. "Six fifty-five to forty-two," he says, depressing the mike button. "I'm parallel to you and turning right on Main. I'll try to get in front of them and block them off."

"Ten-four," 642 acknowledges. "Better snap it up. They're pushing it hard."

As Brogan approaches the intersection of Main and Lake streets, he cuts toward the right. In the same moment, the panel truck approaches the intersection. You can clearly see the startled look on the men's faces as the truck bears down on you, and you hear the protest of tires screaming from both vehicles. You're sure there is going to be a collision, but suddenly Brogan swings back to the left. The panel truck is forced almost to a stop as the marked squad pulls up next to it. In a matter of seconds the truck is boxed in and pulls to a complete stop.

Brogan jumps out of the squad, reaching for his revolver,

42

as the officer in the marked squad jumps out, covering the men with a shotgun.

"Stay down," Brogan warns you. Then he calls out to the men still seated in the truck. "Come on out with your hands up," he orders.

You can see the men step out of the truck, glancing around as if looking for a way to escape. The men are not dressed the way Mrs. Archer and Mr. Summerford described them. They are both wearing blue jeans and colored T-shirts.

"You," Brogan shouts at the man getting out on the passenger side of the truck. "Come around to the front and put your hands up on the hood."

The officer with the shotgun orders the driver to put his hands on the sides of the truck and to push his belly up to it.

Both men do as they're told.

You can see they are in awkward positions, and you realize it would be difficult for them to make any sudden moves.

When the men are in position, Brogan and the other officer approach them, pulling handcuffs out of the cases on their belts. They quickly cuff the hands of both suspects behind their backs, just as another squad screeches to a stop in the intersection, followed by another a moment later.

Jumping out of the squad, you join the policemen grouped around the two prisoners. You can see one of the prisoners is short and stocky with light hair, just as Mrs. Archer described, and the other has dark hair and a slender build. You think they look like the pictures of Jones and Brown, but you can't check because Brogan has the pictures in his pocket.

43

"Miller, you take one of them in your squad," Brogan is saying. "Farrell, you and Billings split up. One of you drive the truck into the police garage. The other can take one of the prisoners."

"Hey, kid, you'd better get back on the sidewalk," one of the uniformed men tells you.

"But . . ." you start to protest as he takes your arm.

Brogan turns around. "It's okay," he tells the officer. "That's my new partner."

The officer releases his hold. "Sorry, kid. I thought you were just a spectator."

Seeing the look on Brogan's face, you decide to head back to the squad anyway.

A few minutes later, the marked squads and the truck are driven away and Brogan climbs back into the car.

"Sorry . . ." you start to apologize.

"Forget it," Brogan tells you, pulling away from the curb. "You didn't goof up. Once they were cuffed, it was okay. The only trouble was, the officer didn't know who you were."

"Yeah," you agree. "I guess I don't look much like a cop—I mean, police officer."

"There's nothing wrong with the word cop," Brogan says. "I use it myself."

"Okay, cop," you reply, laughing. "Do we still show the pictures to Mrs. Archer, or what?"

"Well, you're learning to be a detective. What would you do?" he asks.

"I'd show her the guys we just picked up," you answer.

"You're right. We'll arrange a lineup when we get back to

the station and have Mrs. Archer and Mr. Summerford come down and take a look at them."

"I think they looked like the pictures of Brown and Jones," you say. "Am I right?"

Brogan slips the pictures out of his jacket pocket. "Take a look."

Studying the pictures, you are certain Brown and Jones are the two men who were arrested. "I still think it's them."

"Right again," Brogan says.

As Brogan parks the squad in the assigned space at the station, you can see the panel truck pulling into the garage. You notice the right rear fender is damaged, just as Mr. Summerford described it. "It looks like we've got the right guys," you tell Brogan.

"That's a good bet," he answers. "But we've still got to prove it."

Inside, the men are taken into separate rooms. You can see the one seated in the detective bureau is Brown. He is being guarded by one of the uniformed patrolmen.

Lieutenant Martin calls Brogan aside, out of earshot of the suspect, and tells him something.

"Come on," Brogan says.

"What's up?" you ask, following him out of the room toward the garage.

"We're going to search the truck," he answers. "Lieutenant Martin said he identified the fingerprint we found at the scene of the burglary. It belongs to Jones, the guy that was driving the truck."

"Hey, that's good," you say.

"Yeah," Brogan agrees. "Only so far we haven't got the other one tied in. That's why we'll search the truck before we talk to him. Maybe we'll come up with something."

In the garage, you help Brogan go through the truck, looking under the seats, under the dash, and through the back. It's cluttered with tools, old clothes, shoes, oil cans, a couple of spare tires, and empty beer cans. There is nothing that looks like it could have come from Mrs. Archer's house. "I guess we're out of luck," you tell Brogan. "There's nothing but a pile of junk here."

"Maybe not," Brogan answers, pulling out two pairs of shoes and coveralls from the back of the truck. "These could be the clothes they were wearing when Mrs. Archer and Mr. Summerford saw them. Anyway, we'll get some inked impressions from these shoes and the ones they're wearing. We might get lucky."

Carrying the evidence, you go back into the detective bureau. Brogan sets the clothing on the floor and turns to Brown. "Have you been advised of your rights?" he asks.

"Sure, man," Brown answers. "I already told the lieutenant I don't know nothin' about any burglary. Jones just picked me up a little while ago. Maybe he did something, but not me."

"Whose clothes are these?" Brogan asks, indicating the shoes and coveralls taken from the back of the truck.

"I wouldn't know," Brown answers. "Why don't you ask Jones?"

"I will," Brogan says, picking up the right shoe of each pair. "Take off your right shoe," he orders.

46

Brown pushes his right shoe off and slides it across the floor toward Brogan.

Brogan picks it up and examines the heel, then passes it to you. "What do you think?" he asks.

Examining the heel, you try to recall the design of the heel print that was on the door. It looks similar, but you can't be sure. "I don't know," you answer.

"Let's take all of these shoes into the booking room," Brogan says. "We'll get Jones' too and take inked impressions from all of them and see what we come up with." He turns to the uniformed officer. "Stay with this guy awhile longer," he says.

Picking up the three shoes, you follow Brogan into the booking room. "How come you just want the right shoes?" you ask.

"The print on the door was from the right heel," Brogan answers. "You can tell by the way it was worn on the outside edge on the right side."

Jones is seated in the room, being booked on the burglary charge by Lieutenant Martin.

"Take off your right shoe," Brogan tells him.

Jones takes it off and hands it to Brogan. "I already told the lieutenant I did it," Jones says. "I don't know what you're trying to prove."

"What about Brown?" Brogan asks. "Was he with you?"

"I don't know anything about Brown," Jones answers.

"Whatever you say," Brogan concedes. Then, taking the ink roller from the fingerprinting stand, he spreads a small dab of ink on the glass and rolls it back and forth. When the roller is completely covered, he inks the heel of one of the shoes. Next, he places a clean sheet of white paper on the floor and sets the inked shoe on top of it, then steps on it with all of his weight. A moment later he bends down and removes the shoe from the paper. You can see that the design of the heel has been clearly transferred to it. He repeats the process with each shoe until he has imprints of the four heels.

Prepared comparison chart of heel print evidence, with individual characteristics identified by number.

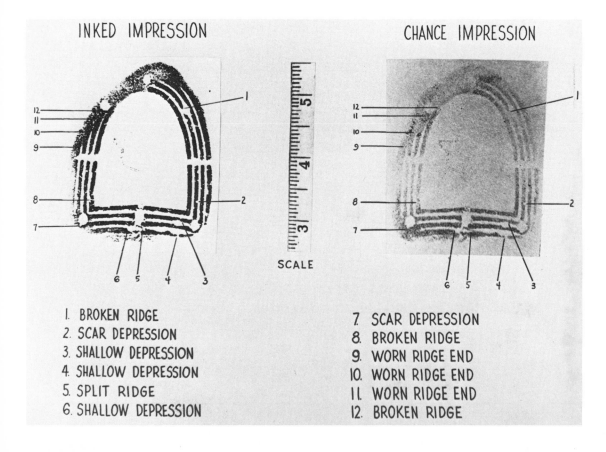

INKED IMPRESSION   SCALE   CHANCE IMPRESSION

1. BROKEN RIDGE
2. SCAR DEPRESSION
3. SHALLOW DEPRESSION
4. SHALLOW DEPRESSION
5. SPLIT RIDGE
6. SHALLOW DEPRESSION

7. SCAR DEPRESSION
8. BROKEN RIDGE
9. WORN RIDGE END
10. WORN RIDGE END
11. WORN RIDGE END
12. BROKEN RIDGE

THE PROOF

"Now we'll see if Fisher's got the enlarged photo of the heel print we found on the door and try to make a comparison."

"But how can you tell for sure?" you ask. "Two of these look exactly the same."

Lieutenant Martin turns to you. "It's almost the same as a fingerprint identification," he answers. "There are many identical patterns; it's the individual characteristics that make the identification. When a pair of shoes comes out of the factory, the heels might have the same design as thousands of other pairs. When a person wears them for a while, he creates individual characteristics in the pattern. He might step on a piece of glass and cut the heel in a certain spot, or scrape it on some sharp object and take off a piece of the design. Just normal wear gives it these individual characteristics that make it different from any other heel print in the world."

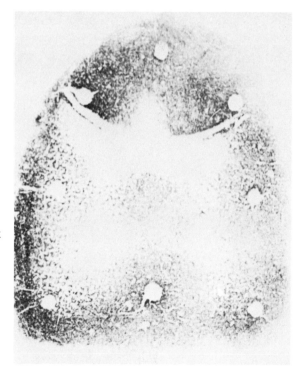

Unidentified heel print found at scene of burglary.

"And you can tell if one of these heel prints is the same as the one that was on the door by those marks?" you ask.

"That's right," Lieutenant Martin answers. "Why don't you check with Fisher and see if he's got the enlargements finished. Try it yourself, then we'll look them over together."

"Thanks, I will," you reply.

You go to the photo lab, where Fisher hands you the finished enlargements. You take them back into the booking room, where you spread them out on one of the empty desks next to the inked impressions of the heel prints. Brogan has numbered the inked heel impressions as one through four and arranged them neatly for your examination. Number one is from the truck, number two is from the shoe Jones was wearing, number three is from the shoe Brown was wearing, and number four was found in the truck.

Can you tell which one, if any, matches? Study the prepared comparison chart on page 48 and note how the identifying characteristics are matched, then try your own examination on the four suspect heel prints. Check the answer section and see if your results are correct.

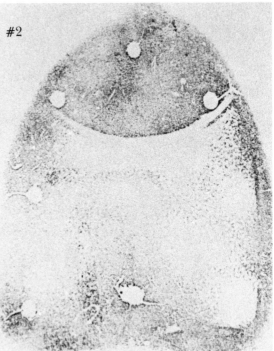

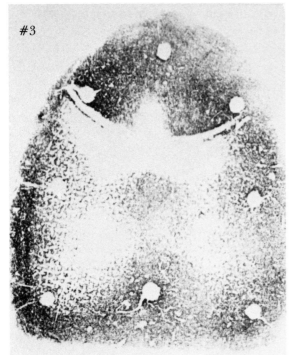

5. A Question of Identity

IT IS AFTER four thirty by the time the examination is completed, and the strange noises in your middle remind you that you haven't eaten since morning. You willingly call it a day when Brogan tells you he will be spending the next couple of hours finishing up the report, fingerprinting and photographing the suspects, and getting the lineup arranged.

Promptly at seven thirty the next morning you report to the station again. This time you go directly to the detective bureau. You find Lieutenant Martin and Brogan seated at their desks.

"Morning," Brogan says. "How does it feel to be responsible for getting the evidence on a couple of burglars?"

"What evidence?" you ask, surprised.

"The heel print, the fingerprint, and the description of them and their truck," Brogan answers. "Mrs. Archer identified them in the lineup, and Mr. Summerford identified the truck. Even Brown decided to give a statement after you left, and we've recovered all of the property out of Jones' garage. So it looks like they're pretty well tied up."

"That's great!" you exclaim. "What happens to them now?"

"They've both been taken to the county jail," Lieutenant Martin answers. "The next step for them is a preliminary hearing to determine probable cause."

"What's that?" you ask.

"It's a hearing where a judge listens to the circumstances of the case. If the accused person can explain away the evidence against him to the satisfaction of the judge, then he is released. If he can't, then he has to stand trial."

"Do you think they'll be able to get out of it?" you ask.

"I wouldn't give them much chance of doing that," Brogan answers. "Still, that's up to a judge or jury to decide. All we can do is present the evidence we have."

Suddenly you hear a commotion in the hallway.

"Wonder what that's all about," Brogan says, getting up to investigate.

You go out into the hallway with him. Two uniformed officers are struggling with a prisoner in handcuffs as they lead him toward the booking room.

"I'd better see if they need any help," Brogan says.

You follow behind, cautiously.

"What's going on?" Brogan asks, accompanying the officers and their prisoner into the booking room.

"We stopped him for not having state license plates on his car," one of the officers explains. "When we asked for his driver's license, he tried to take off, then started to resist us."

You can see the man is about thirty, of average build, with thin light brown hair and a full mustache. He's dressed in

53

brown slacks and a sport shirt. Somehow he looks familiar, but you can't recall where you saw his face before.

"What's your name?" Brogan asks.

"Get lost, cop," the man snaps back.

"Okay," Brogan answers, turning to the uniformed officers. "Empty out his pockets. We'll see if he's got any identification."

Suddenly the man twists violently, breaks away from the two officers, and rushes for the doorway. Brogan grabs the man's arm and quickly pulls him up short, holding him firmly in his grasp as if he were a small child.

"Take it easy," Brogan cautions him.

The officers search the man, but all they find is a package of cigarettes, matches, keys, a few dollars, and some loose change.

"Where's your driver's license?" Brogan asks.

This time, the man doesn't even bother to answer.

"Okay," Brogan says. "I guess you guys might as well lock him up until he's ready to cooperate."

Waiting in the booking room while Brogan and the officers take the man back into the cellblock, you try to remember where you've seen him before. Then it comes to you. The man strongly resembles a picture you saw earlier on a wanted bulletin in the detective bureau.

When Brogan comes back from the cellblock you tell him your suspicions.

"Let's find out," Brogan says. "Show me the picture you're talking about."

In the detective bureau once again, you point out the

wanted bulletin buried beneath a large number of others hanging on a clipboard. The man is listed as Ross Bouchett, age twenty-nine, wanted on a warrant for aggravated battery dated over a year ago. The physical description matches, but the man in the picture has no mustache, and he looks heavier. "I'm not so sure now," you say, looking at the picture closely.

"What's up?" Lieutenant Martin asks.

Brogan explains the circumstances of the traffic arrest and your suspicions. He agrees that the man could be Bouchett. "But," he adds, "the guy is fighting every step of the way. We won't be able to get his prints till he calms down."

"We could dust his car for fingerprints, couldn't we?" you ask. "That way we could find out right away."

"Why go through all that?" Lieutenant Martin says. "We'll get his prints before he's released anyway."

"It wouldn't take long, would it?" you ask.

"It would be one way to find out now," Brogan says.

"Okay, okay," Lieutenant Martin concedes. "If you can't wait, go ahead and dust his car."

The arresting officers point out the suspect's car parked in the police lot. Brogan pulls the dusting kit out of the trunk of the plain squad and carries it over to the car. He removes the jar of black powder and a soft-haired brush, then spreads a light coat of the powder on the glove compartment door, but nothing shows up. He tries the rearview mirror, and this time the clear dark lines of a fingerprint appear.

"That looks like a good one," you say, breathing a sigh of relief as he reaches for a roll of transparent tape from the kit.

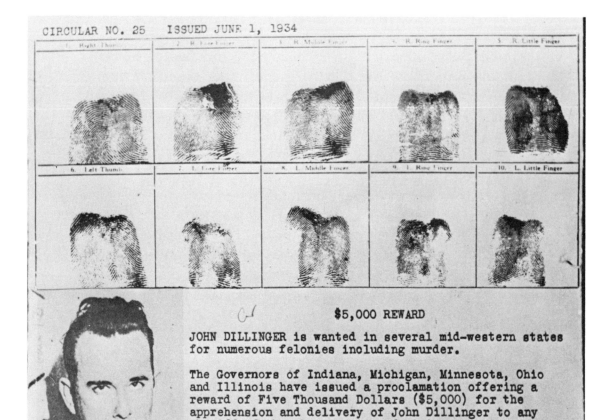

CIRCULAR NO. 25   ISSUED JUNE 1, 1934

$5,000 REWARD

JOHN DILLINGER is wanted in several mid-western states for numerous felonies including murder.

The Governors of Indiana, Michigan, Minnesota, Ohio and Illinois have issued a proclamation offering a reward of Five Thousand Dollars ($5,000) for the apprehension and delivery of John Dillinger to any sheriff of the above mentioned states.

Description: Age 31. Ht. 5'8½". Wt. 160. Eyes yellow slate. Hair medium chestnut. Complexion medium.

Notify any sheriff of Indiana, Michigan, Minnesota, Ohio, Illinois, or this Bureau.

JOHN DILLINGER

John Dillinger, notorious bank robber and killer during the 1930s, thought he could alter his fingerprints through surgery. He didn't realize that nature restores the fingerprint pattern exactly as it was. Though he succeeded in mutilating his fingers, the F.B.I. found over three hundred identifying characteristics in his fingerprints.

"We'll soon see," Brogan answers, laying the tape over the dusted print. Then, taking a plain white index card from the kit, he lifts the print and transfers it to the card. "Take it in and let Lieutenant Martin look at it," he says. "I'll put this stuff away."

Carrying the lifted print into the detective bureau, you examine it closely, but you can't figure out how anyone could make an identification from it. It looks like every other fingerprint you've ever seen.

"I see you found something," Lieutenant Martin says as you walk in and hand him the card. "I've got Bouchett's card pulled from the file. If he's the guy we've got locked up, we'll know for sure in a few minutes."

"I understand how you identified the heel print from the small cuts and wear marks, but how do you identify a fingerprint like this?" you ask.

"Well, you remember how there are many heels with the same design on them that come out of the factory?" he asks.

"Yes."

"It's the same with fingerprints," he explains. "Instead of hundreds of different patterns, though, there are just three basic pattern types of fingerprints that everybody is born with: the loop, the arch, and the whorl." He sketches each of the pattern types on a note pad so you can see what they look like.

"If everybody has these same three pattern types, how can you make an identification?" you ask, perplexed.

"The first step is to identify the pattern type," he tells you. "You can't match a loop with a whorl, or a whorl with an

LOOPS

LEFT-SLOPED LOOP

RIGHT-SLOPED LOOP

ARCHES

PLAIN ARCH

TENTED ARCH

WHORLS

PLAIN WHORL

CENTRAL POCKET LOOP

DOUBLE LOOP

ACCIDENTAL

Lieutenant Martin's sketches of the three basic fingerprint pattern types. Even though the central pocket loop and double loop are called "loops," they are classified as belonging to the whorl group.

arch. It's got to be a loop with a loop, an arch with an arch, or a whorl with a whorl."

"I can see that," you agree. "Then what do you do?"

"Then we've got to look for individual identifying characteristics in the fingerprint, just like the wear marks on the heel print, and try to match them up," Lieutenant Martin answers. "There are seven of these characteristics that are used for identification purposes, although all seven probably won't appear in any one particular print." Turning to a clean page in the note pad, he draws a sketch showing each identifying characteristic.

"For example," he goes on, "suppose you've got an ending ridge in the top right portion of the questioned fingerprint. Then you've got to look at the known print and see if there is an ending ridge in the top right portion of that also. As you continue to look for other characteristics, you might find a bifurcation two ridge lines below the ending ridge on the questioned print. Again, you've got to have a bifurcation exactly two ridge lines below the ending ridge, in the same location, on your known print also. All you're doing is matching each characteristic with another until you've at least eight of them identified. Then you know you have a positive identification."

"Seems kind of complicated."

"Not as complicated as it sounds," he says. "It's sort of like following a street map. If you were to follow Main Street north from Kent Street, what's the first street you would come to?"

"Baker Street," you answer.

59

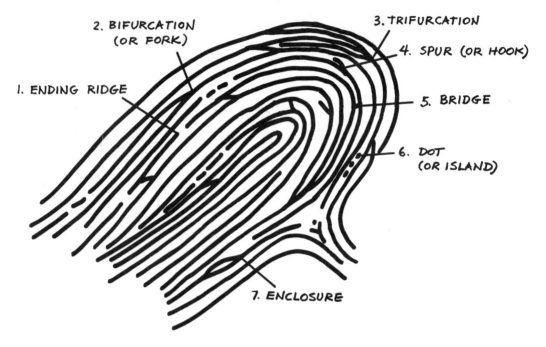

2. BIFURCATION
(OR FORK)

3. TRIFURCATION

4. SPUR (OR HOOK)

1. ENDING RIDGE

5. BRIDGE

6. DOT
(OR ISLAND)

7. ENCLOSURE

Lieutenant Martin's drawing of the seven identifying characteristics.

"Right," he agrees. "But what if the next street wasn't Baker?"

"Then I guess I'd be on the wrong street."

"Right again," Lieutenant Martin says. "It's the same with matching characteristics on a fingerprint. If you've got a bifurcation two ridges below an ending ridge on one print, you've got to have it on the other one also. Otherwise you're on the wrong print. It's not a match."

Latent fingerprint lifted from rearview mirror of suspected fugitive's car.

Right-sloped loops from Bouchett's card.

"I think I've got the idea," you tell him. "Can I try checking the print we got out of the car with Bouchett's fingerprint card?"

"Be my guest," he answers. "If you need any help with the characteristics, just refer to the sketches."

You can quickly spot the pattern types you know won't match, because the latent print is a right-sloped loop and seven of the others are either whorls or arches. There are only three right-sloped loops on the whole card that are possibilities. Still, they all look similar.

When you've examined the lifted print and compared it with the three possibilities from Bouchett's card, decide whether you've come up with a wanted fugitive, or just a balky traffic violator. Then check the answer section.

6. Hit-and-Run

JUST AS you finish examining the fingerprint, Brogan pokes his head through the doorway. "Come on," he calls. "We've got a hit-and-run to cover."

Putting the magnifying glass down, you run out, follow him to the squad car, and jump in. You hear the siren from a fire department rescue squad speeding by, and it seems to make your heart beat a little faster. "How bad is it?" you ask, hoping you won't have to witness a bloody accident scene.

"Don't know yet," he answers, attaching the magnetic mars light to the roof of the squad. The tires screech as the squad leaves the lot. In the street Brogan flips on the switch for the siren to warn the traffic ahead. "Somebody riding a bicycle got hit," he tells you, maneuvering the car around the traffic that is slow in moving over.

Less than two minutes later he slows down, approaching the accident scene. You can see the rescue squad parked with its rear door standing open, the red lights whirling on top. Two marked squads are parked farther down, the beams from their red lights dancing across the roofs of the cars. One of the officers is in the street trying to keep the traffic moving in the other lane.

63

Brogan stops the squad in back of the rescue squad, leaving room for the firemen to move about. Together you walk up to one of the officers on the sidewalk, who is making notes on a pad.

"What happened?" Brogan asks.

The officer points to two firemen carrying a stretcher toward the rescue squad. "Guy on a bike," he answers. "Whoever hit him kept on going."

All you can see is the man's gray hair, his face hidden by a fold in the blanket.

"Got anyone going to the hospital to see if he can tell us anything, and to pick up his clothes?" Brogan asks.

"I was going to go myself as soon as I finish up here," the officer answers. "I don't think he'll do much talking though; he was unconscious when we found him."

The firemen load the stretcher into the back of the rescue squad, and a moment later the wail of the siren sends a shiver down your spine as the squad moves off.

With the ambulance gone, most of the spectators start to drift away. The two officers are taking measurements of the scene for the accident report.

"Why do you need the man's clothes?" you ask Brogan.

"Well, if we get the car and driver, we might find fabric on the bumper that we can match to the victim's clothing to tie it in as the hit-and-run car," he answers. "But right now I'm going to get pictures of the scene."

As Brogan moves around, shooting pictures from different angles, you decide to search the roadway for clues. You spot a few broken pieces of glass and a small fragment of metal, but they look useless. You stop searching and watch Brogan until he finishes.

"Come on," he says, "let's get the bike and load it into the trunk of the squad."

Stepping off the shoulder of the road and across a shallow ditch, you can see the bike lying in a crumpled heap. The rear wheel is twisted out of shape and the frame is badly bent. It's easy to see it was hit hard. You start to bend down to pick it up, but Brogan stops you.

"Hold it a second," he says, kneeling to examine the rear fender of the bike. "Looks like we've got something here." He shoots a close-up picture of the rear fender.

"What is it?" you ask.

Reaching into his pocket, Brogan removes a sheet of paper from his note pad and folds it into a small envelope. "Chip of paint," he answers. "Must be from the car that hit him. At least we know it's tan."

Carefully, he places the paint chip in the envelope and folds it again before putting it into his jacket pocket. "Okay, let's put the bike in the trunk now, then we'll check the area."

"What are we looking for?" you ask as Brogan ties the trunk lid to keep it down on top of the bike.

"The transfer theory, remember? Anything that can give us a clue about the car that hit him."

"Yeah, but how are you going to get fingerprints or anything like that?" you ask.

"I don't expect to," he answers. "We're looking for clues

that were left by the car—pieces of glass, paint chips like the one on the bike, things like that."

"Oh," you say, remembering the glass fragments you spotted. "How about a piece of metal?"

"That too. Anything that can give us a clue to what kind of car it was. From there we can start trying to trace the car and the driver."

"Well, I did find some glass and a piece of metal up the street," you say. "I just didn't think it was any good."

"I'm glad you told me. Remember, you never know what might be the essential clue that clears up a case. Anyway, show me where you found it."

Brogan photographs the pieces of glass and the metal fragment before picking them up. Then you both continue the search for additional clues with no further luck.

On the way back to the station with the bike and the evidence from the scene, you tell Brogan it looks like a hopeless case.

"No case is hopeless," he answers, "until you give up on it. Some might have more and better clues, but you've got to work with whatever comes up, not just the easy ones."

"Sure," you agree. "Only where do you start on something like this one? Nobody saw anything. We don't even know what kind of car it was."

"Not yet, but we do have some clues," Brogan says. "First, since the bike was on the right side of the street and was damaged in the rear, we know that the man was riding in the same direction as the car was traveling. Next, we know that the car must also have damage, more than likely to the right front, because of the condition of the bicycle and the broken headlight glass you found on the right side of the street. We've also got the metal fragment and a good paint sample."

"But how can a paint chip or a piece of metal be of any help?" you ask.

"If the paint chip is from the original factory paint job, the F.B.I. laboratory can tell us what make and year of car we're looking for. We can show the metal fragment to the auto dealers and garage owners in town, and they might be able to tell us what kind of car we're looking for. We can ask them to report any tan cars with right front damage that are brought in for repairs. In the meantime, we can alert all of the squads in the city to look for a tan car with damage to the right front and a broken headlight. If we find it, we might identify it from the paint fragment, the broken glass, the piece of metal, or all three items of evidence."

"I guess it's not as hopeless as it looked," you reply.

"No," Brogan agrees. "But there's still a lot of work to be done."

Back at the station, Brogan removes the bike from the trunk and brings it inside. He places it in the room used for storing evidence and tags it with his name, date, and report number. Then he sets the glass, metal fragment, and the envelope with the paint chip on his desk, identifying them in the same way.

"Let's go check with the officers that handled the accident," Brogan says. "Maybe the guy was able to give them some more information on the car that hit him."

You head for the front complaint desk, where one of the officers is talking to the desk sergeant.

"Find out any more from the guy that got hit?" Brogan asks.

"No," the officer answers. "Riley called from the hospital. He's still unconscious."

"Doesn't sound good," Brogan says.

"No, it doesn't. Riley said the doctors are working on him now, so he's coming back in with the guy's clothes."

"Well, we haven't got much yet," Brogan continues, turning to the desk sergeant. "Until we find out what make car we're looking for, you might have the squads look around for a tan car with right front damage and a broken headlight. We'll start checking garages with a piece of metal we picked up. Maybe somebody can give us the make of car from it."

"Okay," the sergeant says. "Tan with right front damage, broken headlight, make and year unknown."

"Right," Brogan answers. "And when Riley gets back with the guy's clothing, have him fill out an evidence form and turn the clothes over to the county crime lab."

"Okay. Give me a copy of your report as soon as you get it typed up, will you?"

"Sure," Brogan answers. Together you return to the detective bureau.

"How come you're sending the guy's clothes to the county crime lab and the paint chip to the F.B.I. lab?" you ask.

"Because the F.B.I. lab is the only one big enough to have paint samples of all the different makes of cars that have been manufactured in the United States over the years,"

Brogan explains. "Our lab can handle most examinations, but they just aren't as well equipped for some things. Still, using our own lab has the advantage of getting us the answer quickly when we need it."

"Be nice if we could find out what kind of car it is right away."

"It would narrow the search all right," Brogan agrees. "Some things just have to wait, though. Anyway, I've got to finish this report," he goes on, sitting down at his desk. "When I get done we'll grab a sandwich, then see if we can find out what kind of car we're looking for."

You can see by the wall clock that it's almost noon. But the morning has disappeared so fast you hadn't realized it was lunchtime. Still, the offer sounds good. "It's a deal," you answer.

After lunch, you ride around with Brogan, checking with the car dealers, garage owners, and service station attendants, trying to determine the make of car from the metal fragment. It's slow and unrewarding. Brogan explains the nature of the investigation at each stop and leaves his card, asking them to call if any tan car with right front damage is brought in for repair. None of them have any idea what kind of car the metal fragment came from because it's too small.

Finally, just as it's near time for the end of your shift, you pass a junkyard filled with old, wrecked cars. "Why don't we try that," you suggest.

"Good idea," Brogan says. "We haven't had much luck with the garages."

Brogan pulls the squad into the junkyard and goes into the

office. You survey the jungle of metal, stretching almost as far as the eye can see. It looks like it would be impossible to find one car.

A few minutes later, Brogan comes out of the office, followed by a man dressed in greasy coveralls, chewing the stub of a cigar. "Try down that way," the man says, pointing down a gravel road jammed with wrecks. "There's some sixty-eight Chevys down there. I'm pretty sure that's what you're looking for."

"Thanks," Brogan answers, beckoning to you.

Joining him, you walk the road together, looking for a '68 Chevrolet.

"Do you think he knows what he's talking about?" you ask. "None of the garagemen were able to tell you; how could he?"

"I don't know," Brogan answers. "But don't sell the guy short yet. Some of them have been taking cars apart for so many years they could build one from scratch out of used parts."

A hundred yards down the road you spot a '68 Chevy with the front end still intact. "Here's one," you tell Brogan, pointing it out in the pile of junked cars.

Brogan kneels in front of the car, holding the metal fragment at eye level as he examines the trim around the headlight. "Could be from this trim," he says.

"It's kind of hard to tell," you say.

"Here," he says, handing you the fragment. "Look for yourself, see if you can tell where it would fit."

When you've made your examination, decide if you've got a match. Then check the answer section.

7. The Hunt

ON THE MORNING of your last day, you report to the station again by seven thirty, anxious to find out if anyone has found the hit-and-run car during the night. Your comparison of the metal fragment with the trim from the '68 Chevrolet revealed that the junkyard operator was right. But the important thing was, you found out the make of car you were looking for and narrowed down the search considerably.

As you walk into the detective bureau, you spot Brogan and Lieutenant Martin relaxing with a cup of coffee.

"Morning," Brogan says.

"Morning," you answer. "Anyone find the hit-and-run car yet?"

"Not yet," Lieutenant Martin tells you. "That's your assignment for today. I want that car and the driver if you've got to search every lot, garage, and parking area in this town."

"How about the guy who got hit? Is he any better?"

Neither Brogan nor the lieutenant answers your question. The lieutenant turns to his desk, flipping through some papers, as if he'd just remembered he had some work to do.

"What's the matter?" you ask.

"He's still in a coma," Brogan answers.

Brogan drinks the last of his coffee and gets up from his desk. "Come on," he says, heading for the door. "We've got a lot of work to do."

In the squad, neither of you speaks about the accident, but you know it's on Brogan's mind as much as yours. Pulling into a large factory parking area, he cruises slowly up and down the aisles of cars, stopping near every one that fits the description to check for damage to the front end. None of them seems to fit. Some have damage but are rusted, and it's easy to see the damage is old. Some have dents, but none of the trim or glass is broken. After checking each car, Brogan pulls out of the lot.

The search continues through lot after lot for a solid three hours. Finally, the routine is broken as the call number 655 comes over the radio.

"Answer it," he says.

You grab the microphone out of the glove compartment and put it close to your lips. "Six fifty-five, go ahead," you answer.

"Six fifty-five, see the attendant at Mike's Shell, Thirty-third and Carter. He has some information for you."

"Ten-four," you answer, replacing the mike. "Isn't that one of the service stations we checked yesterday?" you ask.

"Yeah. Let's hope he's got some information on the hit-and-run," Brogan replies, pulling the car out of the lot.

A few minutes later, Brogan pulls the squad into the service station drive. The attendant comes out and walks around to the driver's side. "I think I've got something for you on that car you were looking for," he says, resting his elbows on the window frame. "A woman came in about fifteen minutes ago and wanted her right headlight replaced. Said somebody backed into her. Anyway, I fixed it up for her. Then after she left I remembered about the accident."

"What kind of car?" Brogan asks.

"Tan, sixty-eight Chevy. What makes me think it's the right one, it had the trim next to the headlight busted up. Looks like it could fit with the piece you showed me yesterday. And the damage looked fresh."

"Do you know her? Has she ever stopped in before?" Brogan asks.

"Uh-uh. I mean, I think she's stopped in before, but I don't know her. She was kind of young, maybe twenty-five, dark brown hair."

"How about the sealed beam you replaced? What did you do with it?"

"It's in the trash barrel," the attendant tells him. "You want it?"

"Yes," Brogan answers. "If it's the right car, we might be able to match some of the glass fragments with it."

"Hold on, I'll get it," the attendant says. You both climb out of the squad and follow him.

The broken sealed beam is on top of some oil-soaked rags. The attendant hands the pieces to Brogan. "This is all of it," he says.

"Good," Brogan answers. "Anything else about the car you can remember?"

The attendant rubs his chin. "You know, I think the car

74

had a parking sticker on it. If I'm not mistaken, I think it was Ganzer's, the outfit that makes the plastic dishes."

"Good work," Brogan says, taking the broken glass. "You might have solved our case for us."

"Forget it. Anytime I can help," the attendant replies. "Anyway, when Larry gets back from the parts house, I'll check with him. Maybe he knows the woman."

"Okay, thanks again," Brogan answers. You return to the parked squad and take the evidence back to the station.

Brogan places the broken sealed beam on his desk, then gets the pieces of glass from the evidence room. He tries to fit some of the fragments together with the pieces recovered from the service station. In a few minutes he has it matched and taped together. The fit is perfect.

"You've got it!" you almost yell. "It's from the right car."

"Looks like it," Brogan agrees. "We'll take the metal fragment with us and check Ganzer's lot to see if the car is there."

You feel a little tense and excited at the prospect of clearing up the hit-and-run—especially now that you've got the description of a suspect to go on, not just an unknown somebody.

Ganzer's isn't a large factory, and the parking lot holds no more than twenty or thirty cars. In a few minutes, Brogan has checked the entire lot. The tan Chevy isn't there.

"The attendant at Mike's must have made a mistake about the parking sticker," you say, disappointed.

"Maybe," Brogan answers. "But it is noon."

"So what? The car just isn't here."

Sealed beam fragments taped together, showing that each piece fits perfectly with the others. This proves they are of common origin.

"Well, if she went somewhere for lunch, she'll be back in a little while. We'll wait around here awhile in case she shows."

Brogan parks the squad on the street next to the parking lot entrance and leaves the motor running. You watch each car as it approaches, hoping it will be a tan '68 Chevrolet with a damaged right front. Most of the traffic goes right on by, but occasionally a car turns into the lot and parks.

The time seems to drag. Car after car goes by. After a while there is no more traffic into the lot.

"What time is it?" you ask.

"Twenty after," Brogan answers.

"I don't think she's going to show up," you say. "If she went to lunch, she should be back by now. I still think the attendant made a mistake about the sticker."

"Just relax," Brogan tells you. "Waiting is just part of the job. We'll give her a few more minutes."

"Okay. But what do we do if she doesn't show up?"

"Then we'll go inside and ask the personnel manager if anyone of her description—"

"Hey, look!" you exclaim, sitting up straighter to watch a tan '68 Chevy coming toward you.

"Yeah, I see it," Brogan answers. The car slows down as it approaches the lot entrance. As it passes you and turns in, you can see the woman driving. She fits the description the attendant at Mike's gave you.

Brogan pulls the squad out from the curb and follows the woman's car into the lot, stopping behind it as she parks. You both get out of the squad. The woman steps out of her car, glancing toward you questioningly.

"Just a minute, miss," Brogan calls, reaching into his jacket pocket. He pulls out his identification card and badge holder. "I'd like to talk to you."

"What about?" she asks. "I'm in a hurry. I have to get back to work."

As Brogan walks around the squad toward the woman, you move forward to the right front of her car and look at the damaged fender. Part of the trim next to the headlight is broken, and there is a dent in the fender with paint chipped off. There's no doubt in your mind. This is the right car.

"This is it," you call, as Brogan walks up to her on the other side of the car.

She glances at you, then looks back at Brogan. "What's going on?" she asks.

"First, I'd like to see your driver's license," Brogan answers.

Digging into her purse, the woman pulls out a wallet, removes the license, and hands it to Brogan.

"Janice Lorton, Thirteen twenty-nine Caldwell. Is this correct?" Brogan asks.

"Yes, it is. Now, would you mind telling me what this is all about?"

"We believe this car was involved in a hit-and-run accident yesterday," Brogan answers. "But before I go on, I want to advise you that you have the right to remain silent. Anything you say can and will be used against you in a court of law. You have the right to consult with a lawyer and to have a lawyer present with you before you answer any questions. If you want a lawyer but are unable to pay for one, a lawyer will be appointed for you at no cost. Do you understand these rights?" Brogan asks.

"Yes, I do."

"Knowing these rights, do you want to talk to me without having a lawyer present?"

"I don't need a lawyer. Just tell me what this is all about," she answers.

"Look, Miss Lorton," Brogan continues. "We've already

matched some of the glass found at the scene of the accident to the glass that was removed from your headlight unit earlier at Mike's Shell."

"There must be some mistake," the woman protests.

Brogan removes the metal fragment from his jacket pocket. "This was found at the scene of the accident," he goes on, walking around to the right front of the car. "Let's see if it matches the broken trim on your car."

"But I was at work all day yesterday," she says. "Maybe someone took my car while I was working."

Brogan kneels at the front of the car, holding the fragment next to a portion of the trim still attached to the car. In less than a minute he has matched the jagged edge with the broken trim.

"Get the camera from the squad," he tells you. "We'll get a picture of this."

When you return with the camera, he asks you to hold the fragment next to the broken trim, then snaps a picture of it.

"Okay," he goes on, turning to the woman. "Shall we go inside now and see who will verify your story that you were here working at ten yesterday morning?"

The woman turns her face away, wiping her eyes. "Never mind," she answers, her voice choked, as if holding back tears.

"Want to tell me what happened?" Brogan asks.

"It was an accident," she sobs. "I just didn't see him until it was too late."

"Why did you run away?" you ask.

"I couldn't help it. I got scared."

79

When the metal fragment is held next to the trim on the suspect's car, the fracture match shows clearly.

"Sorry, miss. But I'm going to have to place you under arrest," Brogan says. He takes her arm and leads her toward the squad car.

Later, at the station, Brogan fills out the booking sheet, charging her with leaving the scene of an accident. Then he lets her make a phone call to arrange her bond.

When Brogan finishes his reports, you ask him what would happen to the woman if the man should die from his injuries.

"Then she would be charged with reckless homicide, or manslaughter," Brogan answers. "The State attorney would make that decision after reviewing the circumstances of the case."

"Well, anyway, I'm glad it's all over," you say.

"It's not over yet," Brogan replies. "We've still got to prove our case in court. Now, since this is your last day and you won't have to appear in court to prove the case, let's make this your final assignment—helping me prepare the case. See if you can list some ways to help prove she was driving the car and hit the man."

How many can you list? Check the answer section and see if your answers match.

8. The Super Computer

UNLIKE THE ROOKIE DETECTIVE who has a few years' experience as a uniformed officer before getting a crack at the detective bureau, you've had to work under a handicap. The rookie is already familiar with state laws and with constitutional law and has had to deal with people from the angry traffic violator to the man with a gun ready to kill. The trainee has seen what today's detective, with the aid of science and experience, can do—which the detective of thirty years ago couldn't have imagined.

Back in the days of Bonnie and Clyde, Al Capone, and John Dillinger, the police sciences were in their infancy. Many of the squad cars didn't even have two-way radios in them. Investigators had to rely on informants, their ability to recognize wanted persons, and personal ingenuity to capture their quarry.

If the detective of today relied solely on informants and the ability to recognize names and faces, he or she would be ignoring a mountain of knowledge for a molehill of information.

Today, the detective has the National Crime Information Center (NCIC), a computerized bank of information on wanted persons and stolen property, securities, guns, cars,

DEPARTMENT OF JUSTICE, BUREAU OF INVESTIGATION
IDENTIFICATION DIVISION, WASHINGTON, D. C.

Police record on Al Capone, crime czar of the early 1930s. Today the information on this handwritten card would be processed and stored by computer.

and more to assist in investigations. It used to take days to check out a stolen car from another state, because a description of the car had to be put on a list which was mailed out to other police agencies. Now the description can be checked out in minutes by the police officer through the computer. Police resources include the forensic sciences, those sciences dealing with police investigations, which encompass the whole range from chemistry, physics, and biology through the behavioral sciences of sociology, psychiatry, and psychology. A physical anthropologist can determine a murder victim's age, sex, height, and more just from a piece of bone. A dentist can often positively identify a person from a dental filling. A psychiatrist can come amazingly close to describing an unknown suspect from a description of the crime. In almost every field of knowledge there are experts

Detective Bill Knox requesting information from the NCIC.

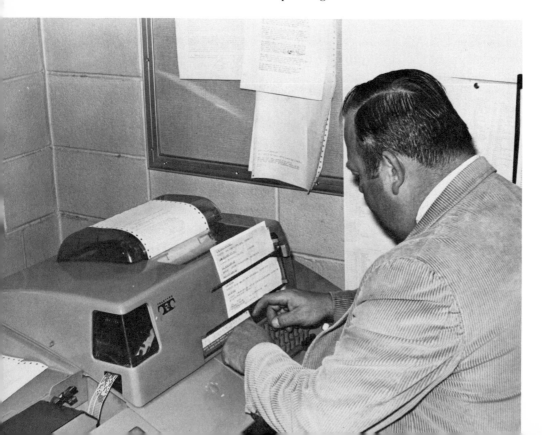

who can help detectives get the most information out of their clues.

It would be impossible for the detective to be an expert in every one of these sciences. It's not even necessary that he or she be an expert in any. Part of what detectives in training must learn is how and when to call on specialists to provide the information they need.

Today's police detective who investigates a crime may be a specialist too—a crime scene technician, who has had training in crime laboratory procedures and techniques. The detective is trained by the experts in local crime laboratories or schools conducted by the Federal Bureau of Investigation to recognize, collect, and preserve the evidence found at crime scenes. The resources of the forensic sciences would be worthless if the detective did not know the value of physical evidence, how to conduct a search for it, recognize it, and preserve it.

And science and technology are only part of the picture. The detective's personal insight and devotion to police work can never be duplicated by a machine. He or she must still develop informants, have a personal knowledge of the local criminals, keep abreast of the constantly changing laws, and relentlessly pursue every challenge, using the best computer in existence—the human brain.

You've had a glimpse of what goes into the making of a detective. If the case problems were fun to work and offered you a different kind of challenge that you enjoyed, perhaps you will go on sometime to be trained as a detective and face problems like these every day.

Answers to Case Problems

1.

1. The crime scene room is the kitchen.

2. The table is rectangular.

3. Did you spot the coffeepot on the small table between the two doors?

4. The unusual object is the pillow. At least, it's unusual to find a pillow in the kitchen.

5. Did you notice the hammer on the bottom shelf of the small table below the coffeepot?

6. If you said there was no knife, you're right.

7. Two doors.

8. Four canisters on the table.

9. Did you notice the third chair? You can see part of the seat and legs under the far end of the table. How about the fourth chair? That's a tough one. Only the bottom portion of the leg appears in the lower left corner of the picture, but it's there.

10. The pillow was thrown on the floor after the murder. Why? Because the smear of blood passes under the pillow in an unbroken line, indicating the blood was there before the pillow.

2.

What made Brogan so sure Lowry wasn't telling the truth? First, how did it happen, if the hole in the pants leg didn't line up with the wound? If Lowry had been walking along as he claimed, the hole should have lined up. But if Lowry had been sitting down, it would explain the difference in alignment. When a person sits down, the pants legs automatically pull up slightly, enough to account for the discrepancy.

Second, where did it happen? The dark area around the bullet hole was powder burn, caused by the weapon being fired at a very close range, probably less than eighteen inches. There would not have been visible powder burns if the shot had been fired from a car pulled up at the curb, three or more feet from the victim.

Why did it happen? According to Lowry's story, there was no reason for the shooting. Even if it had been an act of pure malice, there would probably have been an exchange of words between Lowry and the men, giving some indication of motive.

Finally, when did it happen? The type of crime that Lowry described usually happens under cover of darkness, not in broad daylight where there is a good possibility of witnesses in the area who might furnish accurate descriptions. And Lowry's description was too vague, making it unlikely that he had seen anyone.

When Brogan put it all together, Lowry himself became the suspect, which is why Brogan had to inform him of his rights before going on.

3.

"They're all good suspects," Brogan explains. "But the best ones, I think, are Jones and Brown. The pose they used to case their target is similar to that used by the men who burglarized Mrs. Archer's house. They probably had a truck of some kind, since they were acting as roof repairmen, whereas the other two men either used a car or were on foot. Another thing, Jones and Brown worked together on a job before, but the other ones appear to work alone, since there is no mention of accomplices. The physical description of Jones fits the light-haired, short, and heavy one, and Brown has dark hair and a more slender build like the second one Mrs. Archer described."

4.

If you picked number three, the inked impression from the shoe worn by Brown, you've made a match.

It's easy to see that number one and number four don't have the same class (general) characteristics as the heel print found on the door.

If you studied the area around the center nail hole at the bottom of the heel print, this should be the easiest characteristic to spot and match, compared to the latent.

Moving to the left nail hole on the bottom again, there are two clear lines running straight out from the hole to the side of the heel print.

If you missed these points, a little further study will put you on the right track to find many more identifying characteristics.

5.

If you had a difficult time making a match, don't let it bother you. None of the three prints match the latent lifted from the mirror. In this case, the man wasn't a fugitive, just a balky traffic violator who looked a lot like the wanted man. His inked prints, rolled later, proved he was not Bouchett.

This illustrates the value of fingerprints as a positive means of identification, not only to help convict the guilty, but to free the innocent.

6.

The junkyard operator knew what he was talking about. As you can see, the fragment fits into the section outlined with the dotted lines in the illustration.

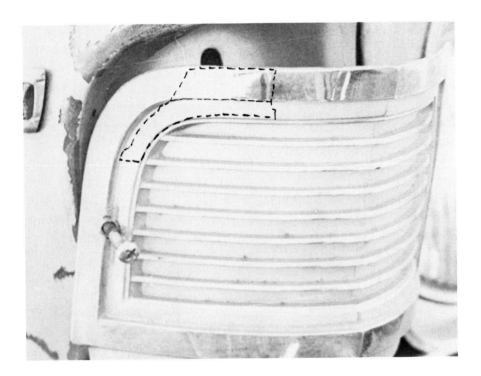

7.

PROOF TO IDENTIFY THE CAR

Paint chip

1. Match by fitting it to chipped area on car.

2. Match by comparing the various colored layers of paint in the chip with those on the car.

3. Instrumental analysis of the paint material itself, showing what it is composed of.

4. Enlarged photograph showing paint chip adhering to fender of victim's bicycle at the scene.

Metal fragment

5. Match by fitting to trim on car.

6. Instrumental and chemical analysis of metal's composition.

7. Enlarged photograph showing fragment was found at the specific location of the accident.

Glass fragment

8. Match by fitting to pieces found at service station.

9. Show fragments came from accused's car by the testimony of the service station attendant.

10. Photograph showing glass was found at the specific location of the accident.

PROOF TO IDENTIFY DRIVER OF THE CAR

11. Her statement, after being advised of her rights, saying, "It was an accident."

12. Her automobile registration showing ownership and attendant's statement showing she had headlight repaired.

POSSIBLE SOURCES OF ADDITIONAL EVIDENCE

13. Blood type comparison, if any traces can be found on the car.

14. Examination of car for any fibers that might have come from the victim's clothing.

15. Examination of car for any hairs that might have come from victim's body.

16. Examination of car for traces of paint that might have come from the bicycle.

17. Finally, to confirm the identity of the driver, Brogan would question the people where Janice Lorton worked to determine when she left work, where she was supposed to go, what route she would most likely have followed, and how long it took before she returned.

If this questioning developed any additional witnesses who could testify to her whereabouts at the time of the accident, their statements would also be taken.

Index

INDEX

About the Author

ROBERT H. MILLIMAKI is in charge of the Detective Bureau of the North Chicago Police Department. The author of *Fingerprint Detective,* he received his training as a detective at the Police Training Institute, University of Illinois, and recently graduated from the F.B.I. National Academy.

PERRY ELEMENTARY LIBRARY

364.12   5.00
Mil Millimake, Robert.
AUTHOR
The making of a detective
TITLE

364.12
Mil Millimaki, Robert.
The making of a
detective

DATE DUE

DEC 30 2001	B		
NOV 19 90			

11TH 45-220